MBIRA
PLAYING

Comprehensive Guide from Beginner to Expert: Explore the Origins, Master Techniques, Embrace Various Styles, Expand Your Collection, and Improve Stage Performance with Pro Tips on Maintenance and Troubleshooting.

SVEN RALF

Copyright © 2025 By Sven Ralf

All Right Reserved

No part of this work may be reproduced, stored in a retrieval system, or transmitted in any form or by any means—whether electronic, mechanical, photocopying, recording, or otherwise—without the prior written permission of the author, except for brief excerpts used in reviews, scholarly analysis, or other instances of legally recognized fair use.

All rights are reserved by the author. For permission requests, licensing inquiries, or concerns regarding rights, please contact the author directly in writing. Unauthorized use or distribution is prohibited and may lead to legal action in accordance with copyright laws.

Published by Sven Ralf

Disclaimer

This book provides general guidance and educational support for learning to play musical instruments. While the techniques and advice can aid in skill development, they are not a substitute for personalized instruction from a qualified music teacher. Progress may vary depending on practice, experience, and correct application of techniques.

The author and publisher make no guarantees regarding the completeness, accuracy, or suitability of the material for every learner. As music education evolves, this book may not reflect the latest teaching methods or research. For personalized advice tailored to your specific goals, challenges, or physical needs, it is recommended to consult a professional instructor.

Safety and Responsibility

Maintaining proper posture, caring for your instrument, and using correct techniques are essential to avoid injury or damage. Always follow safety guidelines provided by certified instructors.

The author and publisher disclaim any liability for harm, loss, or damage—including to instruments, property, or personal well-being—arising from the use or misuse of this book's content. By using this material, you assume full responsibility for your learning experience and agree to prioritize safe and informed practice.

Contents

Inside This Book 10

CHAPTER ONE 13

Introduction 13

Understanding the Mbira: A Brief History and Cultural Significance 14

Why the Mbira is a Unique Instrument for Beginners 16

How This Guide Will Help You Master Mbira Playing 18

CHAPTER TWO 23

Getting Started with the Mbira 23

What is the Mbira? Exploring its Structure and Sound 23

Different Types of Mbiras and Choosing the Right One for You 25

How to Hold the Mbira and the Basics of Posture 27

Tuning Your Mbira for the Best Sound 29

Mastering the Basics of Sound Production ... 31

Creating Your First Notes: How to Pluck the Tines 33

Hand Techniques: Precision and Control 34

Finding Your Rhythm: Basic Timing and Beat Awareness 36

CHAPTER THREE 39

Learning Simple Melodies and Rhythms 39

Playing Simple Scales and Basic Patterns 41

Introduction to Call-and-Response: Connecting with the Music 42

Rhythmic Variations and Developing Your Sense of Timing 44

CHAPTER FOUR 47

Intermediate Techniques for Fluid Play 47

Combining Multiple Finger Movements for Melody and Rhythm 48

Introduction to Ornamentation: Adding Style to Your Play 50

Playing with Dynamics: Using Volume and Intensity to Enhance Your Sound 51

CHAPTER FIVE 55

Practicing Strategies for Consistent Progress ... 55

Setting Achievable Practice Goals 56

Effective Warm-Up Exercises for Flexibility and Strength 57

How to Break Down Complex Pieces for Easier Learning 59

The Power of Repetition: Mastering Each Section 61

CHAPTER SIX 65

Advanced Skills and Expanding Your Repertoire 65

Introduction to Polyrhythms and Syncopation 66

Exploring Traditional Mbira Music: A Deeper Dive into Shona and Zimbabwean Styles 68

Creating Your Own Mbira Compositions and Improvisation Techniques 70

Playing with Other Musicians: Building Harmony and Collaboration 73

Conclusion 76

Reflecting on Your Progress: From Beginner to Confident Player 76

How to Continue Developing Your Skills Beyond the Basics 77

Encouraging Your Own Creative Exploration with the Mbira 79

Final Thoughts: Your Musical Journey with the Mbira 81

Inside This Book

From Practice to Performance: The Complete Beginner's Guide to Mastering Music Skills Quickly with Simple Techniques and Proven Methods for Rapid Skill Development is an essential resource for anyone eager to embark on a musical journey, whether you're picking up an instrument for the first time or seeking to refine your foundational skills. This book offers a step-by-step guide to quickly mastering musical techniques, making it an invaluable tool for beginners who are determined to progress from practice to actual performance. The unique approach lies in the simplicity of the methods combined with proven strategies for rapid skill development, allowing readers to experience tangible results in a shorter time frame.

Have you ever wondered how professional musicians seem to glide effortlessly through complex pieces, or how they achieve such mastery? This guide demystifies that process by breaking down key musical skills into manageable, easily digestible segments. With each chapter, you'll be able to apply these skills in your practice sessions and quickly notice improvements. From understanding rhythm and pitch to mastering the art of timing and dynamics, every essential aspect of musicianship is covered. The book invites you to participate actively by applying these strategies, ensuring that you don't just read about improvement, but experience it for yourself.

What makes this book particularly engaging is its focus on actionable learning. Each chapter is designed not only to explain techniques but also to encourage you to put them into practice immediately. As you work through the sections on topics like finger positioning, breathing techniques, and music theory basics, you'll feel more confident in your ability to progress quickly. The methods outlined have been tested and proven by professional musicians and educators, ensuring that you are learning in the most effective way possible.

CHAPTER ONE
Introduction

The mbira, a mesmerizing instrument with origins deeply rooted in African culture, particularly in Zimbabwe, holds a special place in the world of music. Known for its melodic tones and spiritual significance, the mbira has captivated musicians and listeners alike for centuries. Whether you're intrigued by its soothing sounds or inspired by its cultural heritage, learning to play the mbira opens up a world of rhythmic complexity and melodic beauty.

In this guide, we aim to not only teach you the technical aspects of playing the mbira but also to immerse you in the cultural context that makes this instrument so special. Whether you're a complete beginner or a musician looking to expand your repertoire, the mbira offers a deeply enriching experience. Through this extensive guide, you will learn how to master the basics and begin your own journey into the vibrant world of mbira music.

Understanding the Mbira: A Brief History and Cultural Significance

The mbira is more than just an instrument; it is an emblem of African cultural heritage. Its history dates back over 1,000 years, where it was primarily played by the Shona people of Zimbabwe in religious ceremonies, social gatherings, and storytelling sessions. The mbira is considered sacred in Shona culture, believed to connect the living with their ancestors. The instrument was used in ceremonies such as "bira," where music was played to communicate with the spirit world, making the mbira not only a source of entertainment but also a medium for spiritual communication.

The instrument's construction is simple yet ingenious. It consists of a wooden soundboard (usually made of hardwood) with metal tines (keys) that are plucked with the thumbs and fingers. Despite its simplicity, the mbira produces an intricate and mesmerizing sound, often described as ethereal and trance-inducing. Its music is repetitive, with rich polyrhythmic patterns that seem to transport listeners into a meditative state.

Over time, the mbira has transcended its cultural roots and gained global popularity. Today, the mbira is recognized and appreciated by musicians around the world for its unique sound, its ability to evoke emotion, and its versatility in various music genres. Learning to play the mbira is not just about mastering a musical instrument; it is about connecting with a rich cultural and spiritual tradition that spans centuries.

Why the Mbira is a Unique Instrument for Beginners

For beginners, the mbira is an ideal instrument to learn for several reasons. First, the instrument's compact size and portability make it easy to handle and practice anywhere. Unlike larger, more complex instruments, the mbira can be carried in a small bag, allowing beginners to practice in various environments without the need for much space or setup.

Second, the mbira's musical structure is relatively straightforward for beginners. The metal keys are arranged in a simple pattern, and many mbira songs consist of repeating phrases. This repetition makes it easier for beginners to learn and memorize patterns. With dedication and regular practice, even novice musicians can pick up songs relatively quickly. Additionally, the use of both thumbs and fingers to pluck the keys encourages coordination and dexterity, which helps to develop fine motor skills essential for any musician.

Another advantage of the mbira for beginners is its calming and meditative sound. Unlike instruments that may require loud or intense playing, the mbira's soft and soothing tones make it a pleasure to play, even when learning at a slow pace. This makes it less intimidating for those who are new to music, as there is less pressure to produce "perfect" sound right away.

Finally, learning the mbira introduces beginners to rhythmic complexity in a way that few other instruments can. The polyrhythmic nature of mbira music, where different rhythms overlap and complement each other, teaches students how to develop a deep sense of timing and rhythm. As a beginner, mastering these rhythmic structures will not only make you a better mbira player but also improve your overall musicality across various instruments and styles.

How This Guide Will Help You Master Mbira Playing

This guide is designed to take you through every step of your mbira-playing journey. Whether you are a complete beginner or someone with some musical experience, you will find clear and practical instructions that will help you build your skills progressively. The guide is structured to cover every aspect of mbira playing, from understanding its cultural background to developing the technical skills necessary to perform songs confidently.

Cultural and Historical Context: Before diving into the technicalities, this guide offers an in-depth exploration of the mbira's cultural significance. Understanding the instrument's place in African traditions will provide you with a deeper appreciation of its music and inspire your learning.

Step-by-Step Instructions: Each chapter in this guide breaks down the process of learning the mbira into manageable steps. You will learn how to hold the mbira, the correct thumb and finger positions, and the proper technique for plucking the keys. Each section includes detailed explanations and illustrations to ensure you understand every step.

Music Theory and Notation: For beginners who may not be familiar with music theory, this guide introduces the basic concepts needed to understand mbira music. You will learn about scales, rhythm, and melody in the context of mbira songs, making it easy to follow along and grasp the patterns that make up mbira music.

Exercises and Practice Tips: Throughout the guide, you will find exercises designed to build your skills gradually. These exercises focus on finger strength, timing, and coordination, helping you to play more complex songs as you progress. We will also offer tips on how to practice effectively and avoid common mistakes.

Song Tutorials: Once you have mastered the basics, this guide will introduce you to a variety of traditional mbira songs. Each song will be broken down into sections with clear instructions, so you can practice at your own pace. As you become more comfortable, you will be able to play these songs fluidly, creating beautiful, harmonious music.

Advanced Techniques: For those who wish to take their mbira playing to the next level, this guide also covers advanced techniques such as improvisation and creating your own mbira compositions. These techniques will help you develop your own style and express yourself creatively through mbira music.

By the end of this guide, you will not only have learned how to play the mbira but also gained a deeper connection to the instrument's cultural and spiritual roots. With patience and practice, you will unlock the full potential of this captivating instrument, bringing the timeless beauty of mbira music into your life.

CHAPTER TWO
Getting Started with the Mbira

What is the Mbira? Exploring its Structure and Sound

The mbira, often referred to as the thumb piano, is a traditional African musical instrument with deep cultural and spiritual significance, particularly in Zimbabwe and parts of southern Africa. It consists of a series of metal tines (keys) mounted on a wooden soundboard, with the player using their thumbs and sometimes forefingers to pluck the keys. When plucked, the keys produce a distinctive resonating sound that is both melodic and rhythmic, making the mbira a unique instrument capable of creating intricate polyphonic music.

The structure of the mbira is deceptively simple, but it offers a vast range of musical possibilities. The metal tines are arranged in two or more rows, and each key produces a specific note depending on its length and thickness. A resonator, often a hollow gourd or wooden box, amplifies the sound, creating a rich, full-bodied tone. Some mbiras also have bottle caps or shells attached to the soundboard, which create a characteristic buzzing sound that adds texture to the music.

The mbira is much more than a musical instrument—it is a tool for communication with ancestors and spirits in traditional ceremonies. Its music is often accompanied by singing, clapping, and dancing, and it plays a crucial role in rituals, storytelling, and community gatherings. For a beginner, understanding the deep history and cultural significance of the mbira will enhance their appreciation of the instrument and inspire a deeper connection to its music.

Different Types of Mbiras and Choosing the Right One for You

There are various types of mbiras, each with its unique structure, tuning, and cultural background. The most well-known type is the **Mbira Dzavadzimu**, which is traditionally used in ceremonies to communicate with spirits. This mbira has 22 to 28 keys arranged in two to three rows, and it is usually played inside a resonator, called a deze, to amplify the sound. The Mbira Dzavadzimu is known for its deeply resonant, spiritual tone and is often played in a rhythmic, repetitive manner to induce a trance-like state.

Another common type is the **Nyunga Nyunga Mbira**, also called the "15-note mbira." This version has fewer keys, making it easier for beginners to learn, and it is often used for more secular music and performances. The Nyunga Nyunga is known for its brighter, lighter sound compared to the deeper tones of the Mbira Dzavadzimu. Other types of mbiras can vary in size, number of keys, and regional tuning systems.

When choosing the right mbira for yourself, it's essential to consider both the musical style you wish to play and your level of experience. For beginners, the Nyunga Nyunga is often recommended because of its simplicity and ease of playing. Its 15 notes are tuned in a diatonic scale, making it easier to grasp for those new to the instrument. More advanced players or those looking for a traditional experience may opt for the Mbira Dzavadzimu, which offers a broader range of notes and a more complex tuning system.

Additionally, you should pay attention to the quality of the mbira. Handmade mbiras vary in craftsmanship, so it's important to select one made from quality materials with well-tuned keys. The soundboard should be made of strong wood, and the tines should feel sturdy when plucked. Beginners might also want to look for a mbira with a smoother action on the keys, making it easier to play.

How to Hold the Mbira and the Basics of Posture

The way you hold the mbira plays a significant role in how effectively and comfortably you can play the instrument. Proper posture ensures that you can play for extended periods without strain while also allowing you to produce the best sound from the instrument.

To begin, hold the mbira with both hands, allowing your thumbs to hover over the top row of tines. Your forefingers will naturally fall to the sides of the instrument and may be used to pluck any keys positioned near the bottom. For the larger Mbira Dzavadzimu, your thumbs will pluck the upper keys while your right forefinger is used for the lower keys. On smaller mbiras like the Nyunga Nyunga, your thumbs will do most of the work.

Rest the lower edge of the mbira against your fingers, and balance the instrument so that it feels stable in your hands. If you're using a resonator (like a gourd or deze), the mbira will rest inside it, amplifying its sound. When playing without a resonator, hold the mbira close to your body to enhance the sound.

Your posture is equally important. Sit upright with your back straight to avoid tension in your neck and shoulders. Your arms should be relaxed, with your elbows bent at a comfortable angle. Keep your wrists loose, as this will allow your thumbs to move freely over the tines. It's important not to grip the mbira too tightly—let it rest lightly in your hands, allowing your fingers and thumbs to move effortlessly.

As a beginner, you might find that your thumbs get tired quickly. This is normal, and your muscles will strengthen with practice. Start by practicing for short periods, gradually increasing the time as you build endurance. Focus on maintaining a relaxed, comfortable posture, and over time, you'll develop the stamina needed for longer sessions.

Tuning Your Mbira for the Best Sound

Tuning is an essential skill for mbira players, as it directly affects the sound and harmony of the instrument. Mbiras can be tuned in various ways depending on the type of mbira and the style of music you're playing. The most common tuning system for the Mbira Dzavadzimu is the **Nyamaropa** tuning, while the Nyunga Nyunga is often tuned to a diatonic scale similar to Western instruments like the piano.

To tune your mbira, you'll need a tuning hammer or a similar tool to adjust the length of each tine. Longer tines produce lower notes, while shorter tines produce higher notes. Start by identifying the key that is out of tune by playing each one and listening carefully. Once you find the incorrect note, gently tap the metal tine either upwards or downwards to adjust the pitch. Be careful not to bend the tine too much at once, as this can affect the overall sound quality.

It's important to tune your mbira regularly, as changes in temperature and humidity can affect the tension in the tines. When playing with other musicians or in a group, you'll also need to ensure your mbira is tuned to match the other instruments.

For beginners, tuning can be challenging, so don't hesitate to use an electronic tuner or a reference note from another instrument to help guide you. With practice, you'll develop an ear for the correct pitch and be able to tune your mbira by sound alone. Regular tuning is key to producing the best, most harmonious sound from your mbira, making it an essential part of your practice routine.

Mastering the Basics of Sound Production

Understanding sound production is the first and most crucial step in mastering the mbira. The mbira, a traditional African instrument, produces its unique, calming tones through the vibration of metal tines. These tines are attached to a wooden soundboard, which resonates to amplify the sound.

Each tine is tuned to a different pitch, creating a distinct melodic range that defines the mbira's sound.

To produce sound effectively, it is essential to grasp how vibration, tension, and resonance work together. The mbira's sound quality largely depends on how the player interacts with the tines and the body of the instrument. Whether played softly for a tranquil melody or plucked more forcefully for a dynamic rhythm, each motion creates vibrations that travel through the wooden soundboard, filling the air with the mbira's characteristic hum.

Proper hand positioning, plucking strength, and tine control are crucial elements in producing clear, crisp sounds. Beginners often find that the instrument requires finesse; an overly aggressive approach can lead to sharp, unpleasant tones, while too gentle a touch might result in muffled sounds. Learning to balance plucking strength and sensitivity will enhance the richness and resonance of each note.

Creating Your First Notes: How to Pluck the Tines

Plucking the mbira's tines correctly is an art form that requires patience and attention to detail. Each tine represents a note, and the mbira's unique layout allows players to create intricate melodies by plucking these tines in various sequences. The technique for plucking involves gently pressing your thumbs or fingers down on the tines and releasing them in a quick, controlled motion.

When you first begin, practice plucking a single tine to understand the instrument's feedback. Keep your thumb slightly curved, and use the tip of your nail to strike the tine. It's essential not to rush this process. Take time to become familiar with how much pressure is needed to produce a resonant tone. The angle at which your thumb strikes the tine is also important—plucking directly upward may produce a different sound than plucking at a slight angle.

As you become comfortable, start plucking adjacent tines to create simple melodies. Focus on precision, ensuring that each tine rings clearly without unwanted buzzing or muting. Beginners may often find it helpful to isolate one tine at a time before moving on to full melodies. Building this foundation will allow you to explore more complex patterns as your skill improves.

Hand Techniques: Precision and Control

The art of playing the mbira goes beyond simply plucking the tines; it involves mastering a variety of hand techniques that provide greater precision and control over the instrument. One of the most fundamental techniques is the alternating thumb motion, where both thumbs work in tandem to create a flowing melody. By practicing with alternating thumbs, you will develop a natural rhythm and smoother transitions between notes.

It's also important to develop finger independence. While the thumbs are predominantly used, some mbira players use their index fingers for added control over certain notes or to strike multiple tines at once. This finger-thumb coordination is key to executing more advanced playing techniques, including harmonics and arpeggios.

To develop precision, it is important to focus on hand positioning. The non-dominant hand often helps stabilize the mbira, anchoring the instrument while the dominant hand strikes the tines. The way you hold the mbira affects how efficiently you can control the motion of your hands and thumbs.

Keeping your wrists relaxed and your fingers nimble will allow for greater accuracy and consistency in your playing.

Over time, these techniques will come together to give you complete control over your sound. As you advance, you'll notice improvements in the clarity and dynamics of your music, allowing you to express more nuanced melodies with your mbira.

Finding Your Rhythm: Basic Timing and Beat Awareness

Rhythm is the heartbeat of mbira music, and developing a sense of timing is essential for mastering this instrument. The mbira often functions as both a melodic and rhythmic instrument, meaning that players must keep track of the timing while also focusing on melodic patterns. Without a solid sense of rhythm, even the most beautifully plucked notes can sound disjointed.

The first step in finding your rhythm is to start with a simple, repetitive beat. Tap your foot or lightly count out loud as you play to maintain consistency. Many mbira songs are based on cyclical patterns, where a sequence of notes is repeated in loops. Learning these patterns and sticking to a regular tempo is crucial for creating a cohesive sound.

Once you've mastered a basic beat, begin experimenting with variations. Syncopation, or placing emphasis on off-beats, is a common technique in mbira music. By learning to shift accents and vary the timing of your plucks, you can add complexity and depth to your playing. It's important to listen carefully to how your notes fit within the rhythm, ensuring that the timing is both steady and dynamic.

As you progress, you will start to internalize these rhythms, making it easier to play intuitively. This deeper connection with the beat will allow you to engage with more complex rhythms and play with other musicians, whether in a group setting or in accompaniment to vocals. Developing your rhythmic awareness is the key to unlocking the full potential of the mbira and creating music that moves and inspires.

CHAPTER THREE

Learning Simple Melodies and Rhythms

Playing the mbira, an instrument rich in history and culture, begins with mastering simple melodies and rhythms. These foundational melodies often come from traditional pieces passed down through generations. To start, focus on understanding the relationship between the metal tines and the sound they produce. Each tine is tuned to a specific pitch, and learning how these notes connect is crucial to producing cohesive melodies.

Begin by playing one or two notes at a time, creating a simple melody. As you familiarize yourself with the feel of the mbira, listen to the way the notes resonate. Notice how some notes might blend harmoniously, while others stand out more distinctly. These tonal relationships form the basis of melodies in mbira music. Playing slowly allows you to internalize the sound and timing of each note, developing an intuitive sense of the instrument.

As you grow comfortable with basic melodies, begin incorporating simple rhythms. The mbira, being both a melodic and percussive instrument, lends itself well to rhythm. Start by tapping your feet or nodding your head to the beat while playing a melody. Gradually, this will help you internalize the rhythm and make your playing more dynamic. With time, you'll be able to play more complex rhythms and keep them consistent as you transition between different melodies.

Playing Simple Scales and Basic Patterns

Scales are the foundation of nearly all music, and learning simple scales on the mbira is essential to understanding its full potential. Mbira scales may differ slightly from Western musical scales, but the concept is the same: a series of notes played in ascending or descending order that defines the melodic structure of a piece. Start with a pentatonic or heptatonic scale, which are common in traditional mbira music.

Begin by practicing ascending scales, playing each note in succession from the lowest pitch to the highest. As you do this, focus on accuracy and tone, ensuring each note sounds clear and even. This not only improves your finger strength and dexterity but also builds your familiarity with the note layout of the mbira. Once comfortable with ascending scales, practice descending patterns, playing from the highest pitch to the lowest. This reinforces your sense of the instrument's range and helps develop finger agility.

Next, try incorporating basic patterns that form the structure of mbira songs. These patterns are often repetitive and cyclical, creating a meditative, trance-like effect in the music. Focus on repeating a simple pattern slowly, then gradually increase the speed as you become more proficient. These patterns, when played consistently, become the building blocks for more intricate pieces and can be adapted into different rhythms and melodic lines as you progress.

Introduction to Call-and-Response: Connecting with the Music

Call-and-response is a key feature of mbira music, fostering a deep connection between the player, the music, and often a second mbira player or the audience. It is a form of musical dialogue where one part (the "call") is answered by another part (the "response"). Understanding call-and-response is essential for anyone wishing to immerse themselves in the communal aspect of mbira playing.

To begin, play a simple melody or rhythm, which represents the call. This is typically a short phrase that leaves space for the response. The response can either echo the call or offer a contrasting phrase, adding layers to the music. If you're playing solo, you can experiment with creating your own response, alternating between two different melodies. If you're playing with others, focus on listening as much as playing, responding to the nuances of their call with your musical interpretation.

In group settings, the call-and-response dynamic becomes a conversation between players, allowing for a rich, collaborative experience. This musical dialogue enhances the complexity of the music, as different players might emphasize different rhythms or melodies, creating a tapestry of sound. Learning to balance your call and response with others will improve your ability to listen deeply and react musically in real-time.

Rhythmic Variations and Developing Your Sense of Timing

Mastering rhythm is a critical part of becoming a proficient mbira player. Rhythmic variations bring life and texture to the music, creating movement and energy.

To develop your sense of timing, start by practicing simple, consistent rhythms using a metronome or tapping your foot to maintain a steady beat. As you gain confidence, experiment with subtle rhythmic variations to add interest and complexity to your playing.

One of the hallmarks of mbira music is its polyrhythmic structure—multiple rhythms played simultaneously. Begin by layering a basic rhythm with a second rhythm of a different time signature. For example, you might play a steady 4/4 rhythm on one section of the mbira while introducing a 3/4 rhythm on another section. This creates an interlocking effect, characteristic of traditional mbira playing.

Start by making small changes to familiar rhythms, such as adding extra notes or shifting accents to different beats. Over time, you'll be able to introduce more complex variations while maintaining a strong sense of timing.

This ability to shift between rhythms, speed up or slow down, and introduce unexpected accents will make your mbira playing more dynamic and engaging.

CHAPTER FOUR
Intermediate Techniques for Fluid Play

Once you've mastered the fundamentals of mbira playing, the next step is to focus on achieving fluidity in your performance. Fluid play involves seamless transitions between notes and rhythms, allowing your music to flow without interruption. This is a crucial skill for any mbira player who wishes to take their sound to the next level. At the intermediate level, you'll start to explore more complex finger movements, combine melody with rhythm, and begin incorporating subtle nuances that can bring your music to life.

Fluidity in mbira playing isn't just about speed; it's about control, coordination, and a deeper connection with the instrument. To play fluidly, you must become familiar with your instrument's layout, the positions of the keys, and how each movement you make impacts the overall sound. It requires practicing slow, controlled movements and gradually increasing your speed as you develop comfort and confidence. Let's delve deeper into several key techniques that will help you develop fluidity in your mbira playing.

Combining Multiple Finger Movements for Melody and Rhythm

One of the hallmarks of intermediate mbira playing is the ability to combine multiple finger movements to create complex melodies and rhythms. The mbira, with its unique layout of keys, allows for simultaneous playing of different parts of the instrument. This makes it possible to play bass lines, melodic patterns, and rhythmic accompaniments all at once. To achieve this, you need to develop independence in your fingers, so that each finger can play its own distinct role.

Start by practicing with simple patterns where your thumbs play the bass notes while your index fingers handle the melody. This will help you build coordination between your hands and fingers. As you progress, experiment with different finger combinations—such as using both thumbs for bass and one or two fingers for melody or rhythm. Over time, you'll develop the ability to switch seamlessly between different finger movements, creating a rich and layered sound.

Another key aspect of combining multiple finger movements is syncopation. Syncopation involves playing off-beat or emphasizing unexpected parts of the rhythm. This adds depth and complexity to your music. Practice shifting the timing of your finger movements to create syncopated rhythms, which can give your playing a more dynamic and fluid feel.

Introduction to Ornamentation: Adding Style to Your Play

Ornamentation is the process of embellishing your mbira music with additional notes, grace notes, or flourishes that enhance the overall sound. At the intermediate level, ornamentation becomes a crucial tool for adding personal style and character to your music. These subtle additions can transform a simple melody into something more intricate and expressive.

There are several common types of ornamentation in mbira playing, including grace notes, trills, and slides. Grace notes are quick, single notes played just before a main note, adding a touch of complexity. Trills involve rapidly alternating between two adjacent notes, creating a shimmering, vibrating effect. Slides, on the other hand, involve smoothly transitioning from one note to another, either ascending or descending.

When incorporating ornamentation into your playing, it's important to be mindful of balance. Too much ornamentation can overwhelm the listener and detract from the main melody. On the other hand, subtle, well-placed embellishments can bring out the beauty of the music and enhance the emotional depth of the piece. Experiment with different types of ornamentation in various musical contexts to find what works best for you and the style of music you're playing.

Playing with Dynamics: Using Volume and

Intensity to Enhance Your Sound

Dynamics, which refers to the variation of volume and intensity in music, is another essential element of intermediate mbira playing. By mastering dynamics, you can add emotional depth and expression to your performances. Playing softly can create a sense of intimacy or delicacy, while louder passages can convey strength, excitement, or tension. Knowing when and how to adjust the dynamics of your playing can significantly enhance the overall impact of your music.

To start, practice controlling the pressure you apply to the mbira keys. Pressing lightly produces softer sounds, while more forceful pressure results in louder notes. Gradually work on transitioning between different levels of volume within a single piece. This will help you develop the ability to convey a range of emotions and moods through your playing.

In addition to volume, intensity is another important dynamic element to consider. Intensity refers to the energy or passion with which you play. A soft note played with intense focus and intention can have just as much emotional impact as a loud, forceful note. Pay attention to the way you approach each note, and practice playing with different levels of intensity to explore the expressive potential of the mbira.

Furthermore, dynamics can be used to structure a piece of music by creating contrast between sections. For example, you might start a piece softly, gradually build up to a powerful, intense climax, and then return to a quieter, more reflective ending. This creates a sense of journey and keeps the listener engaged throughout the performance.

By mastering the combination of volume, intensity, and subtle dynamic shifts, you can take your mbira playing to new heights, making your music not only fluid but also deeply expressive.

Intermediate mbira playing requires a deeper understanding of the instrument and a greater focus on technique and expression. By combining multiple finger movements, introducing ornamentation, and mastering dynamics, you can achieve a fluid, captivating sound that reflects your personal style as a musician. These techniques will not only improve your technical abilities but also help you convey the emotional depth and richness that makes mbira music so unique. Keep practicing, exploring new musical ideas, and most importantly, enjoy the journey of musical growth and discovery with the mbira.

CHAPTER FIVE
Practicing Strategies for Consistent Progress

When learning to play the mbira, one of the most crucial elements for improvement is practicing effectively. It's not just about how many hours you put in, but also about the quality and consistency of your practice sessions. A well-structured practice strategy can lead to steady, measurable progress. This involves setting clear goals, using warm-up exercises to prepare your hands and fingers, breaking down complex pieces into manageable sections, and incorporating the power of repetition to master each section fully. Let's explore each of these strategies in detail to help you elevate your mbira playing to the next level.

Setting Achievable Practice Goals

Setting goals is essential for ensuring consistent progress when learning any musical instrument, and the mbira is no exception. However, these goals need to be specific, measurable, achievable, relevant, and time-bound (SMART) to be effective. For example, instead of simply aiming to "improve your mbira skills," you might set a goal to "master the basic rhythm of a particular song within two weeks."

Breaking down larger, long-term objectives into smaller, short-term goals can help you maintain motivation and track your progress. Start with goals like learning a specific song, mastering a certain rhythm, or improving finger dexterity. As you achieve these smaller goals, you'll feel a sense of accomplishment, which will encourage you to keep going. Additionally, setting a regular practice schedule, such as practicing for 30 minutes to an hour each day, will help you stay disciplined and focused.

The key is to challenge yourself without setting goals that feel overwhelming. Pushing too hard can lead to frustration, while setting goals that are too easy may result in boredom. Finding a balance will keep you engaged and steadily improving.

Effective Warm-Up Exercises for Flexibility and Strength

Before diving into playing complex pieces on the mbira, it's important to warm up. Just as athletes warm up their muscles before a workout, mbira players need to warm up their hands and fingers to improve flexibility, strength, and control. This not only prevents injury but also enhances your ability to play accurately and smoothly.

Start with gentle hand and finger stretches to loosen up any tension. One simple exercise is to spread your fingers apart and then bring them back together in a slow, controlled motion. Another useful warm-up involves shaking your hands to relax them and relieve any stiffness. Follow this with finger rolling exercises, where you tap each finger against your thumb one at a time, moving from your index finger to your pinky and back.

After stretching, move to basic playing exercises that focus on dexterity. For instance, practice scales or simple repetitive rhythms that require both hands. This helps improve finger independence and coordination. Gradually increase the speed and complexity of these exercises as your hands warm up.

Effective warm-ups also mentally prepare you for focused practice. By easing into your practice session with deliberate, controlled movements, you're less likely to make mistakes and more likely to play fluidly and confidently.

How to Break Down Complex Pieces for Easier Learning

Mbira music can be intricate and complex, with interlocking rhythms, varying tempos, and subtle melodic shifts. Trying to learn an entire song in one go can be daunting, especially if you're still building your skills. That's why breaking down complex pieces into smaller, more manageable sections is a powerful approach.

Start by listening to the piece as a whole to get a feel for its structure and rhythm. Identify different sections of the song, such as the intro, main melody, and ending. Focus on learning one section at a time, starting with the simplest part. For example, if the rhythm in the intro is relatively straightforward, practice that first to build your confidence.

Once you're comfortable with the easier sections, move on to more challenging parts. Break down difficult rhythms or melodies into even smaller parts. For instance, if a particular phrase is giving you trouble, practice just that phrase repeatedly until it becomes more natural. Isolating tricky sections allows you to concentrate on mastering them without feeling overwhelmed by the entire piece.

Another useful strategy is to slow down the tempo. Play the difficult section at a much slower pace until you can play it accurately, then gradually increase the speed. Patience is key; it's better to practice slowly and correctly than to rush through a piece and make mistakes.

As you become more familiar with each section, begin to connect them. Start by linking two sections together, then add a third, and so on until you can play the entire piece smoothly. This methodical approach will help you build confidence, improve accuracy, and ultimately master complex mbira pieces.

The Power of Repetition: Mastering Each Section

Repetition is one of the most powerful tools for mastering the mbira. By repeatedly practicing each section of a song, you strengthen your muscle memory and develop the ability to play without conscious thought. This frees up mental space to focus on the music's emotional expression and subtle nuances.

When practicing with repetition, it's essential to stay mindful and engaged. Avoid mindlessly repeating the same section over and over without paying attention to mistakes or areas for improvement. Instead, aim for focused repetition, where each pass through a section is an opportunity to refine your technique.

For example, if you're practicing a specific rhythm, repeat it slowly at first, making sure each note is clear and evenly spaced. As you become more comfortable, gradually increase your speed while maintaining accuracy. Repeat the section until it feels completely natural, then move on to the next part.

Repetition also helps you internalize the flow of the music, enabling you to transition smoothly between different sections. Over time, the repeated practice builds up your confidence and ensures that you can perform even the most complex pieces without hesitation.

Consistency is key when using repetition to improve. Practicing a little bit every day is far more effective than cramming all your practice into one long session. By making repetition a regular part of your practice routine, you'll see steady and noticeable improvement in your mbira playing.

CHAPTER SIX
Advanced Skills and Expanding Your Repertoire

As you continue your journey with the mbira, moving beyond the basics opens up a world of advanced skills and creative possibilities. By enhancing your technique and expanding your repertoire, you'll unlock the full potential of the mbira's unique sound. Mastery of advanced techniques will deepen your understanding of the instrument's cultural and musical context, allowing you to create complex, intricate pieces and collaborate with other musicians.

To achieve this, you must focus on two key areas: technique and repertoire. The technique involves refining your ability to play more complex and faster patterns while maintaining precision and clarity. Repertoire means broadening the range of songs and styles you can play, incorporating traditional pieces as well as modern and experimental music.

Learning to master these advanced skills will require dedication, but the rewards are immense. The mbira has a deep history, and by exploring its intricacies, you will gain a deeper appreciation of its role in traditional and contemporary music. Below, we delve into some crucial areas to focus on as you develop your advanced mbira playing skills.

Introduction to Polyrhythms and Syncopation

Polyrhythms and syncopation are at the heart of advanced mbira playing. These rhythmic techniques create a sense of complexity and texture in the music, bringing life and energy to your performances.

Understanding Polyrhythms

A polyrhythm is the simultaneous use of two or more conflicting rhythms. In mbira music, this often takes the form of playing rhythms that overlay and interact with each other in dynamic ways. For example, the left and right hands might play different rhythmic patterns that, when combined, create a new, layered sound. Learning to play polyrhythms requires a high level of coordination and rhythm awareness, but with practice, it becomes a natural and integral part of your music.

Mastering Syncopation

Syncopation involves accenting beats that are normally unaccented, creating unexpected rhythmic shifts that catch the listener's ear. This technique adds excitement and unpredictability to your playing. By experimenting with syncopation, you can transform even simple melodies into more engaging, energetic pieces.

To get started, begin with basic polyrhythms and syncopated patterns, practicing slowly until you can execute them smoothly. Over time, you can build up to more complex combinations, experimenting with different rhythms to create your own unique sound.

Exploring Traditional Mbira Music: A Deeper Dive into Shona and Zimbabwean Styles

The mbira has its roots deeply planted in the traditional music of the Shona people of Zimbabwe. As you progress, it's important to deepen your understanding of these traditional styles to truly capture the essence of mbira music. Exploring traditional songs will not only expand your repertoire but will also give you insight into the cultural and spiritual significance of the mbira.

Shona Spirituality and Mbira Music
Traditionally, mbira music is closely tied to Shona spirituality, where it is used in religious ceremonies and rituals to communicate with ancestral spirits. Understanding this connection will give you a richer appreciation of the songs and their meanings.

Key Traditional Songs and Their Significance
There are many traditional Shona songs that are central to mbira playing. Songs like "Nhema Musasa," "Shumba," and "Chaminuka" have been passed down through generations and are played to invoke ancestral spirits, celebrate life, and offer guidance. Each song tells a story, and as you learn these songs, you are not only learning the notes but also immersing yourself in Zimbabwean history and culture.

Rhythmic and Melodic Characteristics of Traditional Mbira Music

Traditional mbira music is characterized by its interlocking rhythmic patterns and repetitive, cyclical melodies. These patterns are played by multiple mbira players simultaneously, creating a dense, intricate sound. To master this style, you must practice listening carefully to how the different parts interact, and focus on maintaining the repetitive groove that is central to traditional mbira performances.

By delving into Shona and Zimbabwean music, you'll gain a deeper connection to the roots of the mbira and learn how to convey the spirit and energy that traditional mbira music embodies.

Creating Your Own Mbira Compositions and

Improvisation Techniques

One of the most exciting aspects of advancing in mbira playing is the ability to create your own compositions and develop improvisational skills. This allows you to express your individuality while still honoring the traditions of the instrument. By experimenting with melodies, rhythms, and harmonies, you can build new pieces that are uniquely your own.

Developing a Compositional Framework
When creating your own mbira compositions, it's helpful to start with a framework. Begin by choosing a key or scale that you want to work within, and decide on a basic rhythmic pattern to structure your piece. Once you have these foundational elements in place, you can start to experiment with different melodic lines and harmonic progressions.

Incorporating Traditional Elements

While composing original music, it's important to incorporate traditional mbira elements to stay connected to the instrument's roots. For example, using interlocking rhythms or playing variations on traditional songs can provide a solid foundation for your compositions. By blending these traditional elements with your own creative ideas, you'll create music that is both innovative and deeply connected to the mbira's heritage.

Improvisation Techniques

Improvisation is an essential skill for any advanced musician, and the mbira is no exception. To develop your improvisation skills, start by practicing scales and patterns that you are comfortable with, then gradually begin to experiment with variations. Improvising requires a good understanding of the instrument's range and the ability to think creatively while playing. As you become more confident, you'll be able to improvise fluidly, creating spontaneous melodies that add excitement and emotion to your performances.

Improvisation also plays a key role when collaborating with other musicians, allowing you to adapt to different musical contexts and respond dynamically in real time.

Playing with Other Musicians: Building Harmony and Collaboration

Playing the mbira in a group setting offers a unique and fulfilling experience. Collaborating with other musicians, whether they play mbira or other instruments, can help you develop a deeper understanding of harmony, rhythm, and musical interaction. The mbira's complex rhythmic structure lends itself beautifully to ensemble playing, creating rich harmonic textures when combined with other instruments or additional mbira players.

Understanding Group Dynamics

When playing with others, it's important to be aware of the group dynamics. Listening carefully and being responsive to the other musicians is crucial for creating a cohesive sound. In mbira ensembles, players often alternate between leading and supporting roles, depending on the song and arrangement. Learning to balance these roles will help you contribute effectively to the overall performance.

Building Harmonies

One of the most rewarding aspects of playing with other musicians is the opportunity to build harmonies. Mbira music naturally lends itself to harmonic layering, as the interlocking patterns played by different musicians create complex, evolving harmonies. By learning to complement and harmonize with other musicians, you'll enrich the overall sound and take your music to new heights.

Collaborating with Other Instruments While the mbira is traditionally played in mbira ensembles, it also blends beautifully with a variety of other instruments, including drums, guitars, and even electronic instruments. Collaborating with musicians who play other instruments allows for endless creative possibilities, expanding the range of sounds and genres you can explore.

Playing with other musicians encourages growth as a player, challenging you to think outside of the box and adapt to new musical environments. Whether you are performing traditional mbira music or experimenting with modern styles, collaboration will enhance your musicianship and broaden your artistic horizons.

Conclusion

Reflecting on Your Progress: From Beginner to Confident Player

As you reach this concluding stage in your journey of learning the mbira, it's crucial to take a moment to reflect on how far you've come. When you first picked up the mbira, you may have felt unsure, perhaps overwhelmed by its unique tuning, the arrangement of keys, and the complexities of traditional Zimbabwean music. But now, after dedicated practice and immersion in its sounds, you can look back and recognize your growth. From mastering basic rhythms to playing full melodies, you've cultivated a deep connection with the instrument.

One of the most rewarding aspects of learning an instrument like the mbira is witnessing your transformation from a beginner, struggling with finger coordination, to a confident player who can create harmonious, beautiful music. By now, you've likely developed a strong understanding of essential techniques, explored various traditional songs, and perhaps even started incorporating your unique expression into your playing. Reflecting on this journey not only gives you a sense of accomplishment but also provides motivation to keep moving forward.

How to Continue Developing Your Skills Beyond the Basics

While you've made incredible strides in your mbira journey, there is always room to grow. Music, especially traditional forms like that played on the mbira, offers endless opportunities for exploration and improvement. One of the most effective ways to continue developing your skills is to challenge yourself with new and more complex pieces. Seek out advanced songs that require greater dexterity, speed, and rhythmical variation. Practice not only playing the notes accurately but also focusing on the feeling and emotion behind the music.

Another powerful method for development is collaboration. Playing with other mbira players, musicians, or in groups allows you to learn from their techniques and interpretations. Group playing is deeply rooted in mbira culture, especially in Shona ceremonies, where multiple mbira players create intricate layers of sound. By collaborating with others, you can experience new approaches to rhythm and harmony, broadening your understanding of how the mbira interacts in different musical contexts.

In addition, delving deeper into the history and cultural significance of the mbira will enhance your appreciation of its music. Study traditional Zimbabwean music, the spiritual role of the mbira, and the stories behind the songs. This context will not only enrich your playing but also deepen your emotional connection to the instrument, inspiring you to continue evolving.

Encouraging Your Own Creative Exploration with the Mbira

While mastering traditional songs is essential, the mbira is also a tool for personal expression. Encouraging your own creative exploration with the instrument can open up exciting new dimensions to your musical journey. Start by improvising with the scales and rhythms you already know. The mbira is especially suited to improvisation, with its cyclical, trance-like patterns that lend themselves to creative variation. Let yourself explore without the pressure of following a specific song or structure, allowing your intuition to guide you.

You can also experiment with composing your own pieces. Think about the emotions you want to convey and how the unique tones of the mbira can bring those emotions to life. By composing your own music, you create a personal connection with the instrument that goes beyond technical proficiency—it becomes an extension of your inner world.

Moreover, consider blending the mbira with other musical genres. While traditionally used in Zimbabwean spiritual ceremonies, the mbira has found its way into contemporary music, jazz, and world fusion. Try integrating the mbira's sounds into different styles, whether it's accompanying vocals, playing alongside guitars, or even experimenting with electronic music. This exploration will keep your journey fresh and exciting, pushing the boundaries of your creativity.

Final Thoughts: Your Musical Journey with the Mbira

Your journey with the mbira is far from over—it is only beginning. This instrument is not just a musical tool but a lifelong companion that invites you into a rich tradition of music, culture, and spiritual expression. The skills you've developed are a foundation upon which you can build for years to come, expanding your repertoire, deepening your connection to the music, and exploring new creative paths.

As you continue to grow, remember that the true mastery of the mbira doesn't come from playing it perfectly but from the joy, healing, and peace it brings to you and others. Whether you're playing alone or with others, performing traditional songs or experimenting with new sounds, your relationship with the mbira will continue to evolve.

Stay patient with yourself, embrace the learning process, and celebrate every moment you spend with this beautiful instrument. Your musical journey is a deeply personal one, and there's no limit to where it can take you. The mbira will be with you, guiding you through rhythms, melodies, and emotions, helping you discover more about music and yourself with each note you play.